An introduction

When I had the idea for this book, in November 2009, I knew almost nothing about butterflies except that they were very pretty, and I always felt happy when I caught sight of one. Fifteen months on and I have seen almost all of the butterflies in Shropshire, can identify them, some just by their flight pattern, have visited some extraordinary places, have learnt so much about wildflowers, conservation, and their habitats, and have got in touch with the child within, who is not embarrassed to be seen madly racing, twisting and turning, after a small colourful flying insect in the hope of getting a better look.

This book will take you through a year of butterflying in Shropshire. Starting in early spring with the species that have over-wintered as butterflies like the Small Tortoiseshell, Brimstone and Comma butterflies, we meet each of the species as they emerge. Many people reveal their personal encounters, in poetry and in images. You'll find acrylic and watercolour paintings, prints, glass, computer-manipulated images and also sculpture. There are many types of poems, but what they all have in common is an expression of how unique each of the thirty nine Shropshire butterfly species is, and how it can be when we connect with them. The caterpillars (larvae) and eggs (ova) are not forgotten, for even when we can't see any butterflies they are always there, in one form or another - and long may it continue to be so. The book ends in winter, but with the thought of the next spring and the next year's butterflies in the minds of us all. I understand the language of science, but for me, and many others, nothing speaks the truth more clearly than poetry and art.

I had so many wonderful moments with butterflies last summer. What amazes me is that they must have been there all the time. I just hadn't looked before.

I hope you enjoy this book, whether you are a novice or an expert in butterflies, Shropshire, poetry or art. I have certainly loved creating it. And I hope that, after reading and looking at this book, you will enjoy seeing the real butterflies even more than before.

Nadia Kingsley

Shropshire Butterflies

a poetic and artistic guide

to the butterflies of Shropshire

Edited by Nadia Kingsley
Published by Fair Acre Press

Shropshire Butterflies - a poetic and artistic guide to the butterflies of Shropshire

First published in 2011 by
Fair Acre Press
Hunter's Bridge
Newton
Bridgnorth
Shropshire
WV15 5LY

www.fairacrepress.co.uk

Printed by Europrint on recycled stock, using vegetable ink
Cover design: Georgina Pensri

For each book sold there will be a donation made to the West Midlands branch of Butterfly Conservation to support the conservation of butterflies and moths in Shropshire.

Front Cover : Large Heath: Ellen McBride
Back Cover: Dingy Skipper: Lynn Wheeler
Title Page : Meadow Brown: Giancarlo Facchinetti
Acknowledgements Page: Holly Blue: Paul Brooks

Acknowledgements

Roger Garfitt's four poems: *Dark Green Fritillary, Wall, Marbled White* and *Red Admiral* were all written specially for this book.

A Wind from Africa by Gillian Clarke is first published in this book. It was commissioned for the Commonwealth Observance in Westminster Abbey in 2010.

Mario Petrucci's three poems in this book: *Lepidoptera I, Lepidoptera IX* and *Lepidoptera XIII* are all parts of one long poem, published as 'Lepidoptera' in 1999 by K.T. publications as part of the Kite Modern Poetry Series.

Wenlock Edge: This is based on Paul Evans' Wenlock Edge country diary, published by The Guardian on 11th August 2010.

Last chance by Pat Farrington was first published in Orbis, issue 152, 2010.

Common blue by Adrian Moule has shared copyright with Tees Valley Arts, Green TV and Heritage Lottery Fund.

Bird's-foot Trefoil by Neill Webb was first published in BBC Wildlife Magazine, October 2010

Thanks go out to my family, friends, everyone who has shown an interest in this project, and to everyone who submitted work.

.

Many thanks to Roger Garfitt, Mavis Gulliver, Matthew Oates and Mike Williams for their time, encouragement and support, and to Gillian Clarke for so generously giving me her poem at such an early stage.

And thanks to you, the reader.

I would like to dedicate this book to GSF, and to the butterflies.
This book would not exist without either in my life.

In Pursuit of Butterflies

Good, he thinks, to pin them
down. The naturalist
surveys the serried tombs.
Quick life preserved in
patterns for eternity,
kept in line, dead still.

Better to see them move:
light, bouncing, flickering,
unpredictable but held.
The patient camera
fixes movement, stores it,
shelves it in the DVD.

Best get outside. Go walking,
be surprised. Colour erupts.
We are a lumbering rugby pack
wrong-footed, mesmerised
as the fly-half sidesteps, skips away
elusive, fleeting, live.

Small Tortoiseshell

Through winter chill
they rest in the dusk of sheds
the hallowed silence of churches
folded wings hiding
blue-bordered beauty.

When spring sunlight shafts
the gloom
they open like a book
an Illuminated manuscript
of orange, blue and gold.

Beating against glass,
they sap their strength
in futile fluttering,
catch their wings in cobwebs
fade and crumble to dust.

A few fly free
feel the warmth
of a second short summer
fill the future
with the blessings of new wings.

The first butterflies of Spring

A Small Tortoiseshell,
with chequered edge of sloping wings,
blue-spotted lower border, reaches
past the pollen dust
deep
into the nectar of a catkin flower.

Severn sounds its path
through willow roots.
Meanwhile the lone butterfly lifts,
battles against breeze,
masquerades as falling leaf,
down, up, left, then out of sight.

Follow
across grass to the edge of woods
where wind drops low - see
a Peacock glide and swoop,
four monster eye-spots
like its feathered namesake, flash

as it lands on a dead thistle,
briefly basks,
lifts off again.
Soon from nowhere it finds another.
Flutterdancing
they spiral up and up until

gliding down they lie refueling
from the sunshine.
On a lichen-covered honeysuckle sits
a Comma, orange and brown -
like ancient tattered sails its wings.
Soon, in hurried flight

and figures of eight,
it courts another, a mirror image.
A Brimstone flaps across eye level,
large, yellow,
an unerring straight path along the verge.
Walk its route,

stepping over the wood's boundary.
Ignore great tits in oak,
a green woodpecker's shout,
squirrels leaping,
even other humans ...
Keep eye focused on the little.

Brimstone

Brimstone bright yellow
flies fast, free and furiously
looking for a mate.

Comma

flitting low between the jagged margins
>of the orchard **comma** hedgerow **comma** garden **comma**

making a series of brief pauses
>on the buddleia **comma** asters **comma** thistles **comma**

and here it is again thriving amongst
>the currant bushes **comma** hop leaves **comma** nettles **comma**

escaping the butterfly nets and cupped hands **comma**
>taking possession of the air **comma** fluttering out of reach **comma**

>**apostrophe**

becoming an

Comma

Bright-winged,
it skims
(and the meadow sways
around it).
It darts and falters
flashy
Comma orange. It rests
exactly,
on the white plate
of a bramble flower.

Lepidoptera XIII

The poplar is whispering
secrets.   It is Spring.
Among fresh green hearts

the pupa feels the sun.
Its pod splits -
an intimacy of skin.

Fumbling, two legs emerge.
Then a head.   Feathered wires
spring out, sense

magic air.   Now the creased
velvet of wings, awaiting
their thin due of blood.

Viewpoint

Nettles sting and fill a garden
with dilapidation.
Dandelions ruin a lawn and each clock
is its own time bomb.
Thistles scratch bare feet
grow very tall and their roots run so deep
they're hard to weed.
Ragwort kills horses, sheep and cattle
and gives humans a rash when it comes to disposal

BUT ...

in a warm sheltered site you may see
comma, peacock or small tortoiseshell alight
lay egg on nettle
and then take flight.
In early spring
when these butterflies awake
they need nectar fast
find little in imported plants
so imagine their delight when they find a dandelion.
Later goldfinches neatly shred seeds from thistle
but before that butterflies gather
with bees and feed on their flowers.
Ragwort is covered with all kinds of bugs,
they're the sole provider for cinnabar moths,
give their nectar freely to many others,
others who pollinate even our crops.

On seeing the first Orange-tip

Dance with me, in eternity,
Let me dance this life away,
Lead me through the wakened trees
On some perfect April day;
Take me through this ecstasy
Of sunlight beams and stirring breeze,
And lead me to the heart of May.

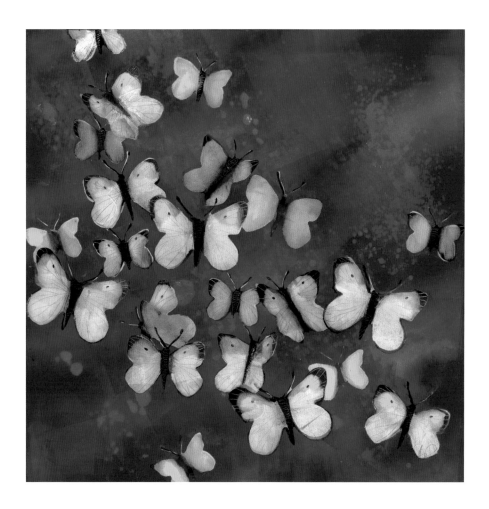

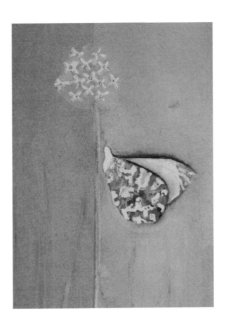

Orange-tip

From sweetly scented honesty and pungent garlic mustard,
to fragile looking cuckoo flower white petals lilac-dusted,
vivid orange and startling white, green marbled underwings,
such energetic dancing flight this pristine beauty brings
to woodland rides in dappled shade and flowery roadside verges,
in amongst the plants from which its larval form emerges.

Holly Blue

Holly Blue in flight
the first blue of the season
likes holly and ivy.

When the attention span is smaller than the wing span…

Flitter, flutter, flitter, fly
I can't remember. Who am I?

Drizzled kipper? Sizzled dipper? Twizzled tripper?
Mizzled quipper? Frizzled flipper? Chiselled stripper!
Oh dear, that can't be right! Fuzzy face; spots of white;
antennae things; earth brown wings.

I'm a GRIZZLED SKIPPER! Yes! Yipee!
A grizzled skipper; that's definitely ME!

Flitter, flutter, flitter, fly.
Doh! It's gone again. Who am I?

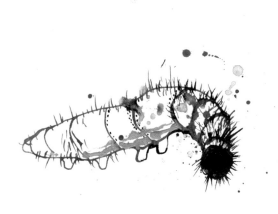

Speckled Wood

From speckled woodland shade
you flicker into passing view,
muted as last year's leaves
that tumbled here in drearer days.

You dance a random path,
shuttle between shadow and sun,
each pulsing pause giving glimpse
of your Brownie-Guide garb.

You journey from bramble to fern,
a puppet on a jerked string,
flicking pollen-freckled wings
like flakes of fallen bark.

You flash your yellow eyes
coquettishly at the world, but,
no painted lady, soon return
to your tree-screened privacy.

Green Hairstreak

Green Hairstreak surprise
needs open grassland and scrub
sole green butterfly.

Green Hairstreak

'The male of the species is territorial
having favourite sites that it uses to wait
for females, but will dart out to investigate
any passing object.
The female, on the other hand,
spends most of her time
searching out nectar sources
and food plants on which to lay her eggs.'

So on Bridgnorth High Street
bikers from Wolverhampton
lounge outside the Tutti Frutti cafe
leathers open to the waist
leering at improbable ice creams
with derestricted eyes
and probing probosces.
Meanwhile pretty as butterflies
in their summer clothes
young mums briefly flutter
outside Tesco One Stop supermarket,
comparing babies and prices
this nappy rash heat wave
before steering their oversized buggies
around the buckled studded calves
stretched laughingly across the pavement ..

Regarding the Green-veined White

In May, I stood corrected: *that's not a cabbage,*
it's a green-veined white, the expert said,

the veins aren't green at all, but
subtle blends of black and yellow scales.

I made a note and took a photograph.
My mistake to think romantic thoughts,

when the yellow-black, called green
but definitely not cabbage white,

flew off and left behind his perfect match,
immaculate if flat against the charlock.

That's your female non-receptive mode,
the expert said, and launched himself into

an exposition on the ins and outs of
reproduction in the green-veined white, and,

by extension, every other member of
the order Lepidoptera. He paused,

before a footnote on Linnaeus
and the proper way to name all living things.

I felt enlightened, though a trifle numb
as if I had been chloroformed, until

I looked around, that Saturday in May,
and saw, pavilioned by the cobalt sky, the air,

from where I stood, to round the Wrekin
and beyond was dizzy with a million aerial pairs,

all wearing well the other names I know:
the bow-ties, motyl, day-flaps, hinges, ghosts,

and what I now could say for certain was
the butter-coloured, green-veined summer-flyer.

Greenfields

I first set eyes on Greenfields one morn at half-past May,
A sense of lushness greeted me that summery-gorgeous day.
Meadows starred with dainty flowers of pink and white and blue,
The verdant scene seemed Eden-like, untouched and sweet with dew.

Blossom-heavy hawthorn boughs whose fragrance filled the air
And tadpoles swam in little pond inviting me to stare,
As here and there flew damselflies and butterflies of blue
Engrossed in such diversity I revelled in the view.

In time I turned, the woods ahead were beckoning to me,
Emanating mossy earth and cool tranquillity.
Up and down the winding path with bluebells ankle deep
Beneath un-stirring canopy, trees seemingly asleep.

The path led to a clearing, bathed in warmth and light,
A butterfly then fluttered by - a busy Green-veined white,
Onwards he flew past Speedwell blue and Buttercups of yellow
With underwings of greenish hue he was a handsome fellow.

Downwards then to sparkling brook, clear waters gently rippled,
Reflected sunlight danced, created shimmer - silver stipples.
The essence of this peaceful scene took hold, began to grow -
I sat in shaded solitude and watched the waters flow.

Dingy Skipper

At the time I thought you too small but since
then I've seen other skippers, Brown Argus,
Small Coppers. I have my eye in now and find
it's the Peacocks and Admirals that are large.

At the time I thought your colour too dull but
now I've seen you flying through your habitat
and noted beige sit well on bird's foot-trefoil
and photographed you to see your marks close-up.

At the time I was happy I could tick you off my list
but then when I let you free you sat on my thumb,
made contact, not just for seconds but minutes as
you travelled with me up the hill. You are the one.

Small Copper

Spark offerer,
you scatter cinders on rudbeckia suns,
those beckoning planets where the border
leans, bees in its flames.

Splay-legged ladybirds
fumbling pollen are stayers-on,
working a flower methodically –
nothing an afternoon;
while you fling beads of heat,
rotate, are gone.

Unpredictable
each shift, fuelled by the embers
of your high-stoked brazier.

The Large Whites' Waltz

In the dance
that is the dance of life
that is the season's song,
nothing is new under our maestro sun
only a summers' novices:
tumbling threes and twos,
fluttering waltzers,
partners to choose and change.

What do they know of *other?*
The wasp who rasps the fibrous
bark of stems; or where he feasts
in plums' warm lanterns;
no tractor revs for harvest,
no buzzard mews for them.

Heat's what they listen to
through powdered wings:
sun, the conductor of all flight.
And they go gaily for the master
in this short waltz they dance to
light on light.

Large White

I`ve got a caterpillar brain
Just like CJ
Trouble is, hers is an Elephant Moth
And mine is not.
When we grow up I`ll be
One of many Cabbage Whites
And she will be an example of beauty
That all will stand in awe of.

Still, at the moment
We both have caterpillar brains

And love each other .

Lepidoptera IX

There are fewer now.

One ate his own support
from under him.   Another hangs
limp and putrid, consumed by virus.

Two others were tried by birds.
Three more died slowly, festooned
with bright yellow cocoons

of *Apanteles glomeratus Linnaeus* -
the parasitic wasp whose grubs
gorge on living caterpillar.

Six fell to hungry earwigs.
Now only four remain, and these
are like estranged brothers.

The third instar is ended.

Gardeners' Dilemma.....with the Small Whites' caterpillars

I give them good deaths – clean –
a quick roll of thumb on leaf –
the cabbage stench.

And there's respect, a knowledge
of the cycle in my head,
how, heat enticed, she dances first
to seek a mate – long light drenched
afternoons, her powdery-fresh wings pale,
endlessly vigorous.

The net barely distracts,
though centimetre mesh to us
might seem impassable;
whatever works inside her
stays the course; one voice alone
her governess.

She'll ease for entry like an infurled sail.

It's all for this – a pause
on underleaf; each fleck's a golden tub
of messages tried over time.
They're on their own, programmed to bulk;
just days it takes high summer: cast skins,
consume down to the cabbage ribs.

I give them good deaths – clean –
a quick roll of the thumb,
naturalist, gardener. Still torn.

Wall

It has come to rest in the language
as it might on a breadth of drystone,
just enough for it to sunbathe on
its own shadow, wings two-thirds open
as the blood heat builds. Will it lift back
into the margin, the hinterland
we take for granted, scrap of colour
that says *sumer is icumen-in*?
(Though it goes back beyond us, goes back
to *vallum*, the Latin for 'rampart',
a word the Saxons or the Anglo-
Frisians *(the Anglo-Frisians!)*
must have found useful as they squatted
among the ruins.) Or will it lift,
wallflower of the fort, little brooch
of the stone, into a place that has
no margins, no time for frippery?

summer summer has come in

summer is

nine muc

Small Heath

You should be in one of those catalogues
for farmers, country loving types, twelve-borers,
those who dress themselves up for horses and dogs,
who ride or stride the land in muted colours.
But you're not one for the four by fours
thrashing above the hedgerows like a lord,
content more with quieter places nearer floors
where summer warmth can hinge you to the sward.
Verges, heaths, dunes, old factory yards or quarries,
you'll settle in any place the feel is right;
until, zig-zagging her catwalk of flight,
she comes to rouse you from your world of snug
(in tweed gilet, moleskin breeks, brown wellies),
and you bring her down with a weightless hug

Pearl-bordered Fritillary

There's an urgency to the male's patrol.
His orange-black wings
take him up and down the rail
they've turned to ideal habitat.
In this moment
his kind are on the rise
but dependent on blue skies
he must mate soon.

The female sits and waits
for pearl-encrusted underwings
to blink on hers. She feeds on bugle.
Soon she flits through dog-violets
then lays an egg.
She'll never know her ink black child.

A Wind from Africa

Was it reading the butterfly book in the garden,
reciting the ordinary poetry of the field,
the lovely litany of *lepidoptera?*
Gatekeeper. Meadow Brown. Small Heath.
Orange Tip. Ringlet. Marsh Fritillary.

Was it a flick of the Gulf Stream's tail, the must
of lion breath, that southern wind that brings
swallows and veils of red Saharan dust
that made the beech tree suddenly wake singing,
flamboyant with uncountable flickering rings
and the almost silent whispering of wings?

The tree dizzy with dancers, manifold,
orange, amber, umber, marigold,
desert reds, trembling Moroccan gold.
Painted Ladies! On a great Odyssey
from Africa, delicate wings on the wind
moving in clouds over continents and seas.

All summer they lingered, feeding, for all we knew
on burdock and the thistles from our fields,
sipping rain, nectar, honeydew.
They live to breed, be beautiful and die.
All winter, ghost butterflies in the tree,
and snow, like white wings falling from the sky.

Small Tortoiseshell

Do not despair.
Extraordinary things are possible.
This dull grub, the glutton,
That gnaws its way
Along a leaf so greedily,
Survives the torture of her adolescence
To become a catwalk beauty,
Supping only on honey
Served in perfumed bowls.

And he, that seemed
A bully, a gross thug,
Is now a ballet star,
Leaping on delicate legs
From bloom to bloom
Ecstatically.

So these harsh hours we suffer
Now, out on the blades
Of the Stiperstones,
Will warm to summer soon,
And crowd with colour -

Just as, on the darkest day,
Love strikes
And leaves you dazzled.

Habitat

They keep the faith, this group of volunteers.
Clear paths, where trailing brambles run berserk,
prepare the way with secateurs and shears
so future boots can carry on the work.
Nettles are worst, like midges: useless pain.
Whether they cut or improvise a flail
the bastards won't give in, but rise again.
That's when a strimmer glistens like the grail.

The aristocrats survey their lush estates.
Red admirals, a solitary breed,
secluded in their tents. The peacocks feed
on nettle tops, uninjured by their stings.
Briefly, a painted lady titivates
before the havoc that the strimmer brings.

Wood White

The wood white sways along the woodland glade
Like a pale shadow. Like a dream
Or an afterthought.

Like that fabled Lady with the Lamp,
Moving through the gloomy corridors
Touching the faces of the wounded.

Wood White butterflies

Risen like brides, tail to tail,
dipping in and out of leaf light,

depositing their gold
beside the Quatt

before becoming snacks
for dragonflies and fly catchers.

Poetry And Peacock

You land on Larkin's *Love Again*
as if it were flowers:
reflective pages
that hand back the sun.

On wind-stirred skirts your ox-bloods
lift and dip; the feat is that you stand
on sheer spun-sugar legs,
your wound proboscis
like a tensioned spring.

This is the closest we can get,
though there's no way our eyes will meet,
butterfly – human. Mine, intent behind
new lenses take you in,
absorbing mock-bold camouflage,
the paints of trick-or-treat.
All empty threats, these mesmerising talcs
rimmed round with kohl.

Not what they seem.

Common Blue
For Olive

Your second summer
eyes wide with wondering
feet eager for adventure
a string of endless questions on your lips.

You danced with butterflies.
Common blues
blue as the summer sky
bright as your smile.

'Blue,' you said, 'blue butterflies',
as you watched them fly and settle,
fly and settle
on the wild thyme on the hill.

Later we saw hydrangeas,
huge heads heavy with blooms.
'Look,' you cried.
'A bunch of butterflies'.

The Uncommon Common Blue

Common was our mothers' greatest fear.
Stilettos, ladders, hemlines hanging down,
haitches dragging in the gutter
made us flighty: made us common.

No-one could say these butterflies aren't *blue* –
blue as relics of the Virgin Mary's cloak;
as sugar bags; Girl Guide uniforms; blue moon;
as scraps of air-mail envelopes.

And suppose they were letters from far-off places –
they'd come with *lots of love* and exclamation marks,
all criss-cross kisses and smiley faces –
nothing there to break a mother's heart.

They can only ever be good news,
these most uncommon of Common Blues.

Common Blues

Keep your lawn longer
grow bird's-foot-trefoil to lure
lovely Common Blues.

Learning Curve

To start with
patterns, colours.
I like that one.
Bright reds, golds, oranges.
White stripe. A brilliant eye
in the middle of a radiant wing.

Next, get the charts
Go out on study days,
meet gurus, pick their brains.
Learn to use nets
transfer to plastic pots
get in real close and photograph
then set them free.

The calendar becomes a timetable
arrivals and departures marked each month.
When to expect a gatekeeper ...
Is this the first or second brood? ...
Anyone seen a clouded yellow yet?

Must get the language right.
I say chrysalis, you say pupa.
Is that an even choice,
a Greek or Latin spinning coin
or is one right, one wrong?

There's only sixty breeds
but if that feels limiting
there's moths.
More than two thousand there,
and most of them no bigger than
your fingernail.

I did once flirt with bats ...

Presences

Level with the Long Mynd
white clouds brush the dark barrow
tent-cloud to war -

The valley, like a Turner
strips back to elemental light,
fields greening lemon-gold, seeded with meadow sweet
cowslip and cornflower,
navigated by flotillas of Brimstone and Clouded Yellows -

Each valley is sculpted, defined
chained like Caractacus and riveted in tree clusters
that threaten to snap and blur in the ether -

Windbreak spinneys of Scots Pine
once storm-tossed in battles
stood their ground in every mound of these hills,
intertwining with beech and hawthorn;

brambles and thistles screening the site
of an old cottage ruin once called 'The Temple'
now guarded by sentries of Dark Green and Silver-Washed Fritillaries
whose flight and fastenings secure their tenancies -

Sheep scatter and pulse, like stars around a white farmhouse
pressing memories where soldiers trod and fell.

Twisting in the fosse, pellets of bone hollow under moss
as tawny Gatekeepers patrol each hedgerow,
while far off and near like ghosts,

white-gold ears of ripening wheat
soften in the distance
to a chenille of waving green.

Stiperstones Valentine

For the Small Pearl-bordered Fritillary

A foggy February drive
via Shrewsbury
then off up through Shelve.
We slide on mud so rutted
it thuds against our undercarriage.

Carrying loppers, saws,
spades, pitchfork, some firelighters,
we squelch through your wet meadow
then past,
to the gorse-rich ground with
woods and more woods beyond.

As the chainsaw goes through
birch, beech and ash,
two wade downstream to make
a natural trough,
others attack gorse then drag
the bodies into fire.

There's no sign of the Exmoor ponies,
nor your over-wintering larvae.

Not knowing if I'll ever see you peak,
or drink in your promised colours,
I imagine a hot soothing bath at home
and how this place might look come June.

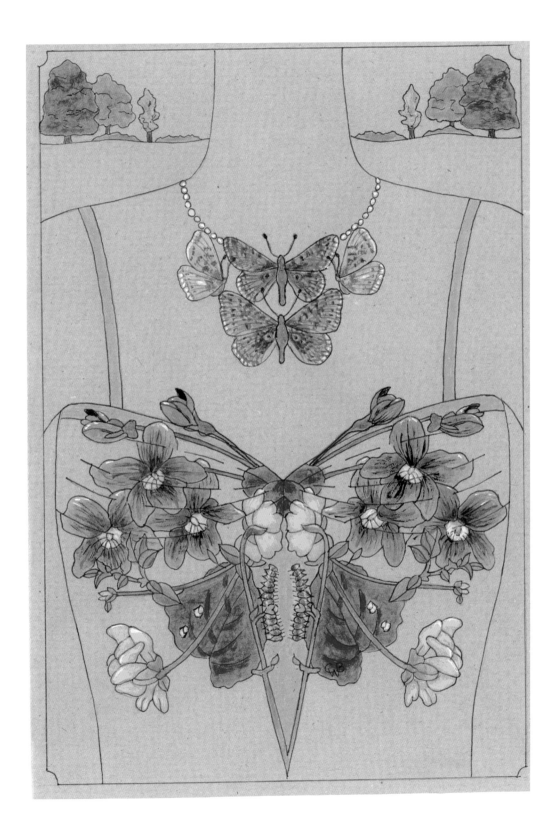

Large Skipper

He sits, spot-lit by rays of sun
that filter through the trees,
his forewings folded at a jaunty angle.
He plays a waiting game
like those lads who stand on street corners
watching all the girls go by.

But he's in no gang. He's a loner.
To him, other lads are competition,
rivals to be challenged, chased away.
If he had fists he'd start a punch-up,
despise the gentle dart and flutter
that's more akin to dancing.

He waits – and when a girl appears
he's instinct driven, off in swift pursuit,
desire to mate his driving force.
The deed complete, back on his chosen leaf
he's an opportunist, watching, waiting,
ready for another one flight stand.

In human terms
he's philanderer, bully boy, chancer,
maybe even a rapist.
In Skipper terms, a prime example of his kind.
He does what Skippers do, sends his genes
winging - into the future.

Meadow Browns' Gathering

We tell fond repetitious tales
like old men hunched on benches:
familiar themes we favour –
tried consensus, you might say;

and leave the rose-cupped scents
to others – let fat flies drown,
reject the fish-hook towering teazles
strewn with Peacock eyes –
choose marjoram.

Next comes our tried routine:
sun lifts and lets us fly
to reach heaven's
purple densities –
forget the blood-lapped poppy,
cornflower scraps of sky;

we choose a humble scent
we nod and chew the fat
we take our time.

Out of Essex

To be known as *small*
or *scarce* was fine,
but then came the Essex tag,
which stuck
like eggs to curled grass.

And with the label
the inevitable titters
amongst the hedgerow flitterati.
Much was made of
Cocks' Foot and Common Couch,
the male's noticeable sex brand,
the amount of amber nectar
necked by gangs of them
socialising in rough pastures
at the weekend.
And then those dumb butterfly jokes.

Perhaps that's why so many left.
Upwardly mobile skippers
skipping town;
spray tan orange clouds
moving up the M1 corridor,
along the verges, heading North.

Dark Green Fritillary

A harlequin's flicker from knapweed
to thistlehead, orange glanced with black
warning enough to stay out of the chase,
the slapstick that will see it mate
in a moment and score twice, a coupled pair
with both heads still drilling for nectar:

but catch it unawares, wings closed
to disclose the green, the furry
underwood green, and it's an old god
you glimpse, who will crawl on his belly
unafraid, who will feed on the dog-violet
through moult after moult to dissolve
into the dark of the pupa, the pulse
where it forms upside-down, folded
energy that can only press into song
or shake out into flight.

Marbled White

Eats its own shell on hatching
secret agent bundling away her parachute

and goes to ground in the grass
wintering on nothing but itself

Grows cautious as the light grows
and feeds only at night

a stem thickening in the Tor Grass
and the Yorkshire Fog

Only to roll as its own dice
on the bare earth   the one

of itself thrown to chance
and come up as wings spread

to the sun   a double six
in a run of luck   and take off

into its variations   move through its
mirrorings to the end

of light

Ringlets

Ringlets in wood glades,
distinguished by outer rings,
love grass and brambles.

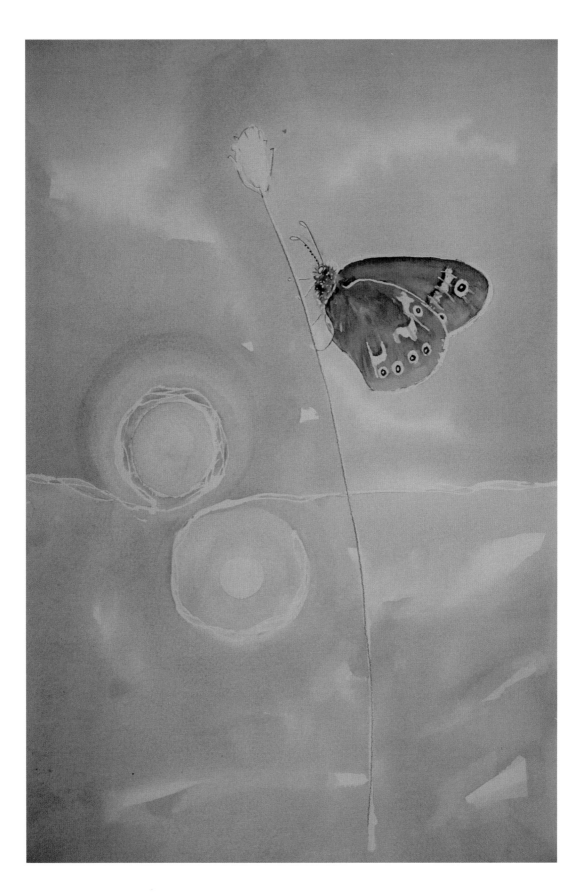

Large Heath

Water drained, peat cut
Bog cotton, long forgotten
Nectar-less, protector-less
Large Heath,
Lay dead beneath

Ditches dammed, enlightened age
Mire repaired, species spared
Nectar fix, on *tetralix*
Much relief,
For Large Heath.

On Whixall Moss ...

Grey pilgrim of the peat hags, wandering the wind
That blows the waste of quivering cotton grass,
Stirring you to rise from nowhere, drift in time,
As midsummer too, arises, sinks and then is passed.

And we must squelch behind you, in hopeless pursuit
Of some perfect image, framed within eternity,
Captured breathless at some place, flowerless and destitute,
That shows you for what you cannot be, a humbled deity.

We were not born for this, you and I, for we were free
Upon the breeze that chimes the endless summer hours,
Above a wasted land of boggy pool and waving reed,
Beyond the pleasantries of budding heather flowers,
Into the passion of the scudding clouds themselves,
Bridging the interstices between two living souls.

White Admiral

The early minutes of
a day observing butterflies.
Lacking experience
I haunt the fringes
waiting, sceptical.

And then this surge.
Enthusiasm pulls
aficionados to the core:
the leader, kneeling, as his net
engulfs a specimen.

Because the others do
I aim my camera at the bulge
and click in digi-hope, knowing
that I can always wipe
one more unprinted flop.

Yet here it is.
No panic, regal in repose.
Through the filters of the net
she lets me see
her colours glow.

The background's warm
rich mottled toffee
but across it cuts
a clear white zig zag line -
Great Wall, from outer space.

Through the lens, the mesh,
the photograph
this radiant courtesan
defies my ignorance
blows me a kiss.

Camilla of the Brambles

Camilla of the bramble flowers,
Sibylla of the woodland rides.

Camilla takes your inner eye
And guides you through the forest,
Her hems are torn and tattered
From her tangles in the brambles, yet
In shafts of sunlit dangling dust
Our lady flies the dappled rides,
And she teaches you to search
Above the bracken and the briars -
There are faces in the foxgloves,
Hidden gods amongst the sallows,
Calling soft from some dimension,
While she slowly weaves her patterns
In your mind.

Silver-Studded

A lone colony, I'm told, the only one in the midlands, in the middle of roads
and noise, the rushing by of everything. How can this possibly survive
without the help of naturalists, some luck, the disinterest of others?

*

And then, there they were, at first
a few weak-flying sapphire blue
or chocolate butterflies scattered

across remains of a war-time airfield,
doing their silver-studded thing;
then hundreds and hundreds floating,

flapping between the heathers,
trefoil and gorse, breath-taking,
idling for a moment, then off again.

And for an hour I watched these blues
their brief lives among the heather,
hiding from wind gusts, bad weather.

*

The walk back is a sobering one; a mix of joy and fear for them,
fear for us, and a vague feeling that only if we care for our children
can sanctuaries like this be kept, be stocked with gems for the future.

The Heath - morning time

Small butterflies blue with wings silver-studded
Emerging in sunshine on heather pink-budded,
Protected by ants whose vigilance brings
Security whilst they inflate crumpled wings.

Prees Heath

Dozens of specks of quick blue,
like tropical fish over coral
in a giant triangular lagoon,
or fragments of summer sky
come down to enchant us all.

One pair, quietly copulating
on a thorny rose twig,
seem superglued together
in uncertain July sun, settled
to display undersides only.

You need a magnifying glass
or a blown-up digital image
to see the male's suffusion
of basal blue, the female's
submarginal silver studs.

Amongst the Heather

Spirits of the heather days
Gathering to dance within
The sun's soft evening rays

Or on some day of endless rain
To hang half-mast upon the stems
Bedecked in pearls, and dance again.

Blues

We been through hard times, blues have had it rough
We been through hard times, blues have had it rough
You plan survival, babe, you better be real tough.

Way back in autumn, yeah, we're knockin' at that door
Way back in autumn, yeah, we're knockin' at that door
Them dumb-ass ant kids now, don't know the score.

Don't know what we're doin', and don't know where we bin
Don't know what we're doin', and don't know where we bin
But they think we their brothers, so they just take us in.

Them ants they feed us, honey, all winter long
Yeah them ants they feed us, honey, all winter long
By the time spring coming, you bet we're good and strong.

Came in as caterpillars, and that's no lie,
Came in as caterpillars, and that's no lie
But when we come out, then we all set to fly.

Our numbers risin' now, and we don't aim to lose
Our numbers risin' now, and we don't aim to lose
So we got no more reason to sing these blues.

Hedge Brown

You are the gatekeeper intent on defining
The line between this field and that with your
Fickle kisses.

Caressing a leaf so briefly the hedgerow
Must yearn for you to return
And touch it again.

Pause and just be still.

The sunlight does not reflect off the flesh
Of the blackberry bush.
Glut of absences.

The Gatekeeper

At Ironbridge I watch the Tollgate,
I need to pay my own debt but have no money to spend.
Travellers are a solemn bunch but still likely to offend
and I'm that patient man who has to wait
till the end of the day, when at night a sign will state:
You have reached your journey's end.
The Gatekeeper, or Hedge Brown, you cannot keep him penned,
the butterfly and I share both name and watchful ability to wait,
though, his brown wings often stay in sight,
he's free to go where others haven't flown,
whilst I am tied, as if to Ragwort at my post.

Silver-washed Fritillary

Two hours on as we
trudge back
down the woodland ride
she visits us
searching for brambles
or violets - so large she's
from when
the dinosaurs walked
the earth - so bright
she's a brilliant
rainforest
orange - so close
we see
her camouflage,
and then
she's off
looping and swooping
her strong flight
ahead
of our stumbling running.
When she takes a
vertical path by an oak
we know
our moment is gone.

Lepidoptera I

At first she ignores him.
Tripping
over scented air
her coiled proboscis darts in and out
of the sweet throats of honeysuckle.
Mites run up it like mice.
Playing
hard to get, she lets him hover
just above her.   He wafts
a wash of pheromones
across buoyant antennae.
He is tireless.
For hours
he winks and flutters
thus sparkling
colours no other eyes can see
shedding
a golden rain of scales,
each dentate flake laden
with the chemical imperative.
She is intoxicated.
Gradually she acquiesces,
settles like a leaf
on a twig.
They copulate
then part
like leaves caught in a scud.

Purple Hairstreak

Thistles spur the meadow in July
unpack their blazoned heads.
The oaks are crowned
with honeydew and the air-
dance of this colony,
indigoed, extraordinary.

You tell me
you've seen them flutter down
to drink the dew
on the woodland ride, and
bathe
their changelings.

Who's to say?

Evening Flight

Where the evening sky hangs still,
Shafts of July sun stretch softly
Warm along the wood edge oaks;
Living dust ascends within the heat,
In particles, miasmic and opaque,
To greet the climax of the day;
For there, just there, entirely there,
Within the sun's last radiance,
Grey sprites of frenzied vibrancy
Circle-dance the living air,
In celebration of Midsummer's days;
Engulfed within the moment that is all
And everything to those in courtship
Of a life beyond an evening of eternity.

Then pray, my spirit, deftly pray
That you might join the dance of Psyche,
And these small butterflies that worship her
In tones of iridescent purple and of humble grey,
Before they drift into the forest night.

White Letter Day

First find an elm,
A stately tree, once common
In hedgerows and city streets
Until an incomer
Brought death in its wake.
On a fine June day,
Fragments of leaf,
Brown against the sky
Flit between branches,
Or rest, camouflaged on bark
Unseen above the heads
Of most walking by.
Look up;
Among the canopy of elms
Dances a small papillon
Its hind wings marked
By a white letter W.

White Letter Hairstreak

Likes the top of trees, a speck in the sky,

one brood every year towards the end of July,

see the white lines from which it gets its name and

the streak of an underbelly 'W', no pattern the same

early morning flights in search of honeydew,

never far from Elms, gathering nectar to renew,

females always looking for a quiet place to lay,

settling for a moment then off on their way

never still with open wings

hairstreaks are elusive things.

Grayling

Leave me alone, I say.
Let me be
dark as crumbled peat
grey as winter heather
pale as sunstruck limestone.
Let me blend in
wherever I happen to find myself
on slate scree or salt dune.
Let me become near invisible
having no vote, no opinion.
Let me sit here appearing smaller than I am
frizzled wings tucked in
easy to overlook
streaked like marram
speckled like granite.
Frightened, I flare
up a forewing - flash of orange fire,
black eye roundelled as if in anger...
But mostly I hide, I cower.

Now I am beginning to disappear
I wonder: will you be sorry
(will you even notice?)
when my camouflage becomes
nothing but background for ever?

On Llynclys Common

For Marion & Bill

Light cloud drifts slowly across the sky
this August afternoon and browns
are out in force,
                          glide from knapweed
to thistle,
              from harebell to self heal,
while common blues seek out trefoil
& small coppers cling to ragwort.

This field is filling up with bracken
but between the grasses flowers
are a mass of yellows, blues and purple.

The last few pyramidal orchids
turn from powder pink to plum,
nod towards the summer's end.

Hover flies gather around the yarrow,
under the hawthorn rabbits sniff
the air for stoat or fox.
                          We take
some photos, walking to the gate,
leave everything as found.

Red for Danger

Brown Argus, be aware, that this sunny
August day is not just about you
finding a mate or laying your eggs.

As you bask on ragwort flower know
that this farmer is obliged by law
to stop the spread of your nectar favourite.

So, by orange-spotted wings of brown
fly like quicksilver out of this trap
back to your home on chalk. For you

are so small you won't be missed. He
knows his business. It is ideal weather for
spraying. He needs it done before harvest.

September butterfly

I hadn't realized
a butterfly
could feast on blackberries,
could sink
proboscis through the
silk thin skin
and drink
juice, like a horse,
head lowered
at a stream.

As in a dream,
a dust of brown and amber spread
across the soft black cluster,
smudging close-clinging globes.

It cast a tint,
a hint of shades
the trees are only now
imagining,
as slightly tired leaves
plan the music
for their funeral.

A passing fly, a cloud
or wind catching the bush,
and this flash
of Autumn colours
shuts, like a door
bringing dusk.

For a moment it hangs,
quivering, grey-brown,
like last years leaf
clinging fast to the last
to its source of life;
then shivers and rises effortlessly
to float high, bright
into the blue
sky.

Last chance

Homing in on my hand, it lands
delicately tickling my skin,
dark edges round its broken wing.

All-seeing eyes grip mine, strangely
unafraid, so near I become aware
of countless hairs on spidery legs.

Curling antennae press against the air,
but its body rests, feet trusting my thumb,
the prow of an ark.

To A Meadow Brown

Who renders ordinary,
who judges plain?
You, without Peacock magic,
Eastern promises: rose and lemon
powders for the eyes.

As summer beckons rot,
dead leaf yourself,
you blow through autumn rides
wearing drought's watermark,
smudged fingerings of ash:
frail ornament enhanced
by subtle silts.

The Peacock Winged Ones

Not for us to know
what beckons bee-heat
to the bright meniscus of the butt,

it simply calls them
and they answer. Like flies
to privet's sweaty liquors
from the poison chest.

So, you leave cups of roses
to the hoverflies, though
they are sumptuous;
whole skies of cornflowers
cannot tempt, or the enamelled gloss
of poppy skirts.

Teazles are yours,
you clip its cones and sip:
a dowager who takes her tea
and eyes the fancies:
just so the limbs,
just so the little finger.

You are no flighty girl
despite your kohls,
despite those sweetmeat eyes'
doubling keep-off camouflage.

You bask,
compressing down for sun,
display your peacock patterns
and survive.

Red Admirals in September

Black-red, red-black beats from a windfall plum.

The admirable sips sweet ooze and flutters up.
Our casual awe infuriates the blue-tit
swooping for an air-snatch. He shrieks fury.
She flies to nectar on sedums, Michaelmas daisies,
and waits with wings closed on a whitewashed wall.

Her hind-wings mimic bark, chipped brick,
her forewings scraps of singed print from old bonfires.
She flies again where buddleias poke out tongues.
Her wings fan; autumn's fires are slow to kindle -
blue summer lasts and lasts.

She's winking, flirting, making a shadow-play
on baked stones, warming her muscles for flight.
The blue-tit strikes again.
She's languid on the up-flutter, lures him high,
and freefalls through barring twigs.

Near sunset a male lands on the west window.
The hairs on his busby body beat constantly,
his open wings stain the glass: red bars, white and a dot of cobalt.
The transfer is imperfect; a veteran of aerial combat -
he's clipped like a train ticket —

and travels on.

Red Admiral

We never dreamed they were gypsy colours,
those bands of red where earth brown
shades into black and black
flashes white and has a sheen of blue.
We never saw *tzigane* in that orange hem.

Someone would shout 'Red Admiral!'
and it was as if an ensign were flying
beyond the ring of marbles or the first
conker fights, a cutaway from history
you could catch and cup in your palm,

the trembling of its wings a kiss
like Hardy's, an initiation
into the band of brothers. You hesitated
to let it go, to become a star on the chest
or a bloodstain on the quarterdeck.

We never suspected it had flown out of
its own deep song, the innate impulse
that sent its forefathers north in the spring,
Roma who would mate over the ivy clumps
of a new island. Or that those colours

unfurled from a tent in the nettles, those zags
of red flickering over the apples we scrumped
from back gardens, would have to be struck
against the trunk of a tree, the bark of
its underwings turn ghostly in the frost.

Small Tortoiseshell

I don't know who first named you

the Small Tortoiseshell

or why it caught on.

Watching you posing on the buddleia now

it doesn't do you justice.

You could be

the Mandolin –

for your wood veneer sheen

and your delicate fretwork wings.

Try the Marmalade –

for your bitter-sweet orange glow

rich and radiant in the sun.

Or the Tiger Leopard –

for your terrifying tawnyness,

your trick with spots and stripes.

You could be a Fluted Wedgwood –

for those fancy pale blue chips

scalloping your wing-tips.

Or even the Small Blue Fingernail –

your unexpected fashion statement,

your modest impulse buy.

And now you've closed your wings

to mystify your predators -

you look just like a Freckled Pond Sludge.

How can a name

net you, hold you, pin you down?

There you go, with your fumbling

trembling wing-flaps

wobbling over the fence,

whoever you are,

Small Tortoiseshell.

Imago

Like

a Red Admiral without a fleet,
a Painted Lady out of lippy,
a Large Heath that's been built on,

a White-letter Hairstreak on a red-letter day,
a Small Skipper without a rope,
a Purple Emperor sent into exile,

an Orange Tip with a dose of the blues,
a Gatekeeper replaced by automatic barriers,
a Brown Argus when the fashion's for black ,

a Brimstone without a spark of fire,
a Grayling forced to work in colour,
a Ringlet cut by a kid with scissors,

a Small Copper with a duff arrest rate,
a Comma missing the rest of its sentence,
a Small Tortoiseshell without an occupant,

a Wall rammed by a stolen car,
a Marbled White who's lost its marbles,
a Silver-studded Blue with an allergy to metal,

so am I
without you.

From the Hibernaculum of the Small Skippers

December sun drops behind border hills.
The thermometer retracts its red line
through minuses towards the bulb.

In woodland clearings, along roadside verges,
straws of summer's waving grasses
fold under snow. Deep in sheaths,

amongst the tatters of Yorkshire Fog,
False Brome and Timothy,
the caterpillars hibernate in silk-spun air.

A few grasses spike the crystal crust
beside hogweed's spokes, knapweed's
burnt-out beacons and the rusty lances of thistles.

My mind skips seasons to animate
golden-orange butterflies fluttering
through high summer -

fast-forwards to dizzy flits through
purple passages of betony, scabious, thistle.
Memory races with adults through their days

of courtship, nectaring and basking
wings half-closed, as they half-rest,
perched on tall grasses, poised to dart

and defend territories. Males oust invaders
as the female probes the right
ripe stalk to encase her white eggs.

They will hatch before days shorten,
spin and tie tight,
to out-silk storm and frost.

Small Tortoiseshell

In December you are spread on my carpet,
dropped down from somewhere into the room,
your rich Tyger-Tyger animal pattern
scorching a dull, flat grey far from nature.
I select a small book from my shelves,
open its covers to create a shovel,
and as I ease the thick card beneath you
your wings snap together in a single twitch.
Miles from summer, and many more until spring,
it is not the time or place for your story.

Seasonal

In the slow programmed wrinkling down to seed
butterflies have no part, not bound
to pods of knowing freight;

not theirs our word late-summer
blown in to take them unawares:
dense surreptitious cloud
whose layers halt their flight.

Only their sensing of it – the result.

They close like summer paper backs
shelved without sun, clasp
to a sheltering plank,
a tent of bark, and sporting
dusty jackets against frost –
held, camouflaged
they hunker down.

Winter releases them as frass
on mad March wind,
or faded, battle-worn, to snatch
at April's inhospitable reprieve.

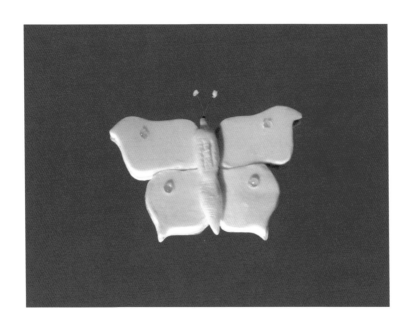

Brimstone

Often I've been cheered
on a hard frost-steaming day in March
turning over the clay with a heavy heart
to see you so early up and about
winging it here and there like a child's dab
of sunshine with your orange spot.
Or on a late October evening
sipping the last of purpleness
from the tired old greys of a buddleia.
The first to arrive.
The last to depart.
Is it because you have learned to hibernate
twirling closed up like a green-veined leaf
in ivy tod or cobwebbed shed?
Is it because you have learned to wait
out the cold, the disappointment,
that makes you such a welcome star?
'Yellowbird' some call you, tilting your wings
at right angles to the best of the sun, -
no talk of dying out for you, my friend.
Original butter-coloured 'fly',
heartening as a first primrose
glimpsed along the hard-edged way.

Wenlock Edge

Squirrels are at the unripe hazelnuts already
and rowan berries are pillar-box red. Last week the berries were
the same rich amber colour as silver-washed fritillary butterfly wings.
There's something cultish about the fascination for fritillaries. Far
from being all fey and fragile, these butterflies are big, beautiful
and powerful. They can fly between ground-level and treetop in
seconds. When they cross beams of sunlight in woodland clearings
they have a presence which immediately fixes my attention and
something triggers a chase mechanism so that, even by eye, there's
a moment when my whole being feels as if its running after them.
Perhaps that's a legacy of butterfly-chasing as a child but perhaps
it's a more atavistic impulse to hunt treasure. The way fritillaries
move illicits the chase but the sight of them at rest is also a reward
in itself. In an open woodland glade on a bank of old limestone spoil
covered in grasses, black knapweed, wild basil, pyramidal orchids and
hare bells, many butterflies were making the most of the sunshine and
the air was full of their strobing brown, gold and white wings. Then a
couple of silver-washed fritillaries showed up and the atmosphere changed,
becoming charged by an electrifying charisma. Somehow their
snapping flight filled the space of the clearing and then they landed
on carefully selected dark purple knapweed flowers to feed. As they
did so their wings opened and undulated sexily, drawing nectar but
also presenting strange black markings which looked like glyphs
written across the orange-brown wings. On the undersides flashed
panels of mother-of-pearl which gave them the 'silver-washed' moniker.
They are woodland creatures belonging to an ancient enchantment
between light and shade; their caterpillars feed on violets which adds
to their romance. These are animals which seem to bear the insignia
of an alien intelligence, inhabiting our world cryptically, showing themselves
but briefly.   Paul Evans   95

Prees Heath and the Silver Studded Blue

In the 1970s, as ploughing began to make inroads into the heath, I saw the Large Blue. I think it only fair to say that every expert I've spoken to, tells me that I am – or was – mistaken, but I am comforted by the testimony of the commoners: they saw it too.

I'm not a butterfly specialist, but like many children of my generation, I had my Observer Books, and my sister and I were, in our amateur way, experts. Jenny Joy, who did research on the heath into the symbiotic relationship between the Silver Studded Blue and ants, assured me I was mistaken. But I could have sworn ...

> *Even as we speak of it we see the harebell*
> *loose flight from chiming petals: a silent applause*
> *as the wings lift, stretch their astonished metamorphosis*
> *in blue wonder. We have no words – a miracle,*
> *wafer on the tongue, blue whisper over the heath.*

By the time I was commissioned to write about the heath in the mid 80s, the Large Blue had disappeared. It was as if it had shrunk. The Silver-studded Blue was there in considerable numbers – despite the encroachments of agriculture, and the woodland that was gaining a foothold.

It was Geoff Saum, the last commoner to graze his cattle on the heath, who first posited to me the idea that if the Butterfly Conservation Society took an interest in the butterflies, that in itself could save it. And it is thanks to the untiring efforts of the commoners and local people, and their enterprise in enlisting the interest and support of Shropshire Wildlife Trust and Butterfly Conservation, that the habitat of the Silver-studded Blue on Prees Heath has been assured.

For the non-specialist, the process of restoring the heath to its pre-First World War status sometimes seemed obtuse. Local people saw the little copses being felled, and wrung their hands: but the heath is back now, and the heather and broom thrives. The occasional Silver Birch hangs on in there – they feature on post cards from the early 19th Century – but the trees cannot be allowed to burgeon as some would have liked. Heathland butterflies don't thrive in woods.

There are winners and losers. The gypsies, who used to stop over since long before living memory, no longer find access to the heath. Their absence is something I regret, but, apart from a few families who have earned the respect of commoners and locals alike, the travellers are not welcome. Some of them have broken faith with the land. As one of the gypsies told me, *There's bad ones that leave a mess. There are bad ones everywhere. Not just on the road.* But part of the heath's magic has gone with them – the smoke rising from the fire, the red roof of a caravan, the horses that seemed to be tethering the heath, reinforcing its fragile hold on the landscape. The comings and goings of the gypsies were part of the life of the heath, part of the eco-culture which sustained not only butterflies, but partridge, duck, wild swans, geese, rabbits, foxes, badgers, and a vast variety of wild birds which the older members of the communities that surround the heath remember with nostalgia.

Overall the heath is shaking itself back into something akin to the natural beauty which used to act as a magnet to visitors a hundred years ago. The movement for the restoration of the heath has overcome every kind of obstacle. The resultant SSSI has seen the return of butterflies in greater numbers. Visitors can expect to see not only the Silver-studded Blue, but many other varieties: small and large white, brimstone, small copper, small skipper, gatekeeper, and meadow brown were spotted on a recent visit. As for my Large Blue ... Well, it's proving elusive.

But I live in hope.

Eleanor Cooke

Farmland butterflies

Visit Melverley Meadows - Shropshire Wildlife Trust's nature reserve near Whitchurch, on a summer's day and you find yourself in the sort of landscape you might have thought had vanished some time in the last century. Meadow Browns, Small Coppers and Common Blues flicker among the tall grasses, orchids and other flowers. These are not rare butterflies, but rarely on farmland do you see them in such abundance.

Over the last 50 years or so, the richly varied pastures and meadows which once provided an exquisite diet of nectar, flower buds and leaves for butterflies at each stage of their life-cycle have all but disappeared. At least 97% of Britain's flower-rich grasslands are reckoned to have gone under the plough or been degraded through overgrazing, fertilisers, drainage and even neglect. So every surviving patch of flower-rich grassland is highly valuable. Every bit of wet meadow with lady-smock or marsh violets is keeping alive the plants needed by Orange-tips and Small Pearl-bordered Fritillaries. Look out for field scabious and the dusky purple flowers of hemp agrimony and you see butterfly banquets on stalks.

These special places are jewels in our landscape and invaluable seed sources for the future, 593 of them are designated as Wildlife Sites in Shropshire. While some of these continue to decline each year, it is Shropshire Wildlife Trust's vision and aim to connect these surviving areas of wildlife interest and to extend their range.

Agri-environmental schemes bring hope for butterflies. Financial support is given for measures such as creation of nectar and pollen grassland strips. Less frequent cutting of hedgerows is also encouraged, which means more flowers and fruit for wild creatures of many kinds. The continuance of such funding is essential for the future survival of butterflies.

For centuries traditional farming practices benefited butterflies by default. Now agriculture has become so efficient the weeds and the wild flowers have all but vanished. Today we must write them into farm plans and work with our landowners, sharing knowledge of how to look after these places – and pay for them too. Can we afford to do this? A world without butterflies would be a grey, diminished old world. We cannot afford not to.

Sarah Bierley

Verge-life

Traffic is my least favourite flavour of jam! I was ensnared in a metal box on the A5, the sun taunting everyone with visions of far more scenic or sophisticated places to be than here. Certainly I had so many more options than this scruffy part of the carriageway (or at least I thought I had!). In desperation I started to scan the roadside verges looking for anything to distract my attention from the squabbling couple with their cola-filled kids in the car in front. Suddenly I spotted several shimmering male Common Blues battling over a large patch of bird's-foot trefoil with its egg yolk flowers on the sloping, sheltered, south-facing verge. *Lotus corniculatus*, the larval food plant of the butterfly and the only 'Lotus' worth having on this road!! The butterflies blazed above the vegetation oblivious to the human column of impatience that silently seethed inside the snake of vehicles by their sides. Suddenly a siren, as blue lights diverted our attention to the human cost at the front of the queue but I couldn't help wondering if the policemen directing gawping drivers away from the carnage, had for a second, had his head turned by the ranked mass of Gatekeepers, those guardians of the hedgerow, who fluttered flirtatiously along the verge. Or whether the knapweed flowers festooned with end of season Meadow Browns had caught the eye of the green clad paramedic at the scene?

Inevitably as broken bones and gouged metal were removed and the little pieces of debris swept away into history the road once more became fluid. All verge-life returned to the blur and fizz of speeding traffic whilst the territorial battles of butterflies raged on without witness or recognition.

Pete Boardman

Gardens and butterflies

I came to Shropshire to make a garden. I knew nothing: I planned to learn as I went along. I began by sowing grass and planting hedges. Then, gradually, as the world within the hedges began to fill with plants and trees and flowers, the wild life moved in — first the birds, spying out the land; then the insects and the reptiles and — more cautious — the mammals. And gradually we got to know one another. But it was years before I knew anything about the butterflies: years before I realised that the butterflies were always there, even when I couldn't see them, present as eggs or larvae or pupae in the unregarded wild edges of the garden, or simply asleep, as adults, dozing away the heat of midsummer in the shade of a garden wall or the long months of winter in the old privy which became my garden shed; years before I realised that there were spring butterflies and May butterflies, early summer butterflies and August butterflies, their emergence pinpointing a mood or a moment in the gardening year as precisely as any flower; that there were yellow butterflies and blue butterflies and orange butterflies, not just the brilliantly coloured butterflies of September and October which I remembered crowding the Michaelmas daisies of my childhood, or the 'Cabbage Whites' against which my father waged war. Brimstones and Orange-tips, Holly Blues and Meadow Browns; Speckled Woods, Gatekeepers and Commas, Small Tortoise-shells and Large Whites, Peacocks and Red Admirals — year by year, as the garden grew, the butterflies kept arriving, weaving their way into my gardening calendar.

The Tortoiseshells of course had always been here, as thoroughly domesticated as tabby cats — in summer breeding on the nettles in the dung-enriched soil where the old pig stye used to be, in winter sharing the house with me. Of all the butterflies, they live closest to man: I am almost never without a Tortoiseshell for company. Sometimes on warmer days in winter they wake from their hibernation and flutter against the inside of the windows of the house, as if to check whether spring has arrived. But it is the Brimstone, outside, flapping his way slowly across the garden like a detached piece of the pale March sunshine, who for me marks the real start of the gardening year. He will have spent his winter asleep among the evergreens in the garden — in the hollies of the Canal Garden or in the tree ivy on the garden walls, or perhaps in my mixed evergreen hedge — camouflaged among the leaves by the smooth greenish sheen of his underwings. Now he emerges, a yellow butterfly, into a world of yellow flowers: celandines and pussy willows, winter aconites and crown imperials, marsh marigolds and primroses.

As March turns into April, the Orange-tips hatch out — the colour of the orange tulips and terracotta pots in the Ivy Garden — followed a week or two later by the first brood of Holly Blues. The Holly Blue is the colour of hope, of fresh starts and new beginnings; of blue hyacinths, pulmonarias, scillas; the time of year when everything's perfect and the world is your oyster — a lovely, light-hearted blue. My favourite time of year; my favourite butterfly. The Holly Blue has two broods a year: the first overwinters as pupae on the ivy, emerging in April; the second will pupate on the holly, emerging in July; and if the females of the first brood are like chips of cool clear April sky, the females of the second brood are like the thundery skies of high summer, their wings a darker violet-blue with broader navy blue borders like clouds shaded dark beneath by the threat of sudden downpour. This is a problematic time in the garden: the July gap, when the roses are over, and the fresh green growth of early summer is beginning to darken and flag; I try to cheer myself up with blue agapanthus, late blue clematis, try to keep the blue campanulas going by deadheading them.

Then three beautiful surprises: the Speckled Wood, with his silvery grey-brown wings dappled with cream. I associate him, like the Meadow Brown, with the more secret parts of the garden, the places of sunshine and dappled shade — the shade of trees I planted twenty years ago, suddenly grown huge. And the Red Admirals, who travel thousands of miles to be in my garden: their arrival always a cause for celebration. I discover them with the home-grown Peacocks feasting on the sweet golden flesh of fallen greengages in the Plum Walk. And the 'Cabbage Whites' — even they! — seem to me now beautiful and strange, drifting among the tall stems of the late blue lavender like tiny sailboats on a blue sea.

The Gatekeepers arrive next. They are hedgerow butterflies, and seem to get their name from their habit of sunning themselves on the timbers of five-barred gates. But for me they are gatekeepers in another sense: they are the harbingers of autumn. They arrive in sudden flocks, tawny in the long grass of the Wild Garden, marking the turning of the seasons from high summer to the season of seedheads and stubble fields. This is when I cut the yew hedges and scythe down the Lammas meadow, when spaces in the garden open up again. There's a feeling of relief and release which I always associate with the arrival of the Gatekeepers.

And then the final act, the climax of my gardening year, in September and October, with the Noisette and *Moschata* roses starting to repeat, the apples ripening in the Fruit and Vegetable Garden, and the Michaelmas daisies — powder-blue and blue-violet, deep indigo, red-purple and darkest maroon, covered with great quivering mixed flocks of Peacocks and Tortoiseshells and Commas, haloed about with the busy comings and goings of innumerable different bees and hoverflies, all shimmering gold in the late October sun — just as I remembered them in my father's garden.   Katherine Swift

Reminiscences of 'The Silver-haired Man' :
A Shropshire Old Lad

Norfolk evenings are often warm during August, and are always wrapped in the biggest of skies. Different to those of others in whose blankets have comforted me. No better; no worse.

I'm beginning to forget short-term stuff, like what happened yester*day*, but I can remember events of yester*year* as clearly as Waterford crystal.

Scraping the frost off the inside of my boyhood bedroom window belongs to Salop.

I remember that clearly.

'M'darlin', John's here to see you'.

*****

My pals joined me butterfly and moth-hunting around the Ercall Woods. The Elm trees formed a dense canopy over the shallow pits where once I dug for marbled bottles.

On our way to those dark places, we marched noisily along a track known to us as 'The Path'. A bare, narrow, and probably now extinct, corridor of naked limestone atop the once sweat-stinking kilns of Darby's industrial revolution. The Dingy Skipper flew over them, too, and on so many other days when we explored the foetid caves that yawned beneath us.

Mike Oldfield's Tubular Bells hissed from John's cassette player.

We fought as musketeers, our swords thrashing heroically against the rough foliage. With each thrust fell a blizzard of Clouded Magpie moths. The track was littered with their hopeless wings as confetti on a miserable wedding day. We could not take a step without crushing the pile of their delicate carpet. Never have I seen such a sight. The surface of the Ercall reservoir was solid and silent with their spirits. An exhausted Blomer's Rivulet paddled amongst them. Waiting beneath was the cavernous mouth of a large Chub. It was one of three that lived here. They were the stuff of legend amongst us boys.

I remember them clearly.

******

Arms pumping, and using all the fortitude our PT teacher slippered into us, we chased it. Four inches across the wings, if not a foot. With golf balls raining around us, we caught our treasure on the fairway of the Wrekin golf course. A Monarch butterfly. The only one, perhaps, ever seen in Shropshire.

******

And I remember the drowning White-letter Hairstreak brought to me by Steve, on a bit of tissue paper. He found it adrift on the reservoir's inky waters. What about all those other butterflies we used to see then on our happy hunting grounds? Ringlet, Purple Hairstreak, Speckled Wood, Meadow Brown, Gatekeeper, Common Blue? They were all so common then ...

I wonder if you remember that single Elm tree at the foot of the Wrekin where the male White-letters fenced to our amazement. That once mighty tree is asleep now, casting erotic lights from between their skeletal fingers onto the thirsty Bluebells and hypnotic Ramsons. Somewhere beneath their beds, from cocoons spun amongst the dust, there waits beauty.

****

From beneath the orange reservoir of an impossible Norfolk sky, I remembered John's words about Tubular Bells. *'It reminds me of people and places I shall never see again'.*

Yeah, and do you remember the black dog we saw on the Longmynd, when we were trapping for the Small Lappet moth? In legend, an omen of death. At the end of the nineteenth century, The Rev. Newnham used to write his cape-flapping hellfire and brimstone sermons there between hunting for the county's butterflies and moths ...

Just one more thing, if I may. 'Shall never see again?' I beg to differ. I see you every day in my thoughts.

'Where's your buddy, Hon?'

Oh, I guess he must have left.

Yes, I'm sure I remember that clearly.   Adrian M Riley

A personal perspective on Shropshire Butterflies

Having grown up in Cambridgeshire where there is little left to discover and the islands of good habitat are few and far between, I find Shropshire to be a real gem. It is incredibly under-recorded so everybody undertaking a butterfly survey has a real chance of turning up a new colony of something important - perhaps one of our most rapidly declining butterflies such as the Small Pearl-bordered Fritillary or Dingy Skipper. Habitats which are rare in other parts of the region can still be fairly common and widespread in Shropshire such as rush pastures, unimproved grasslands and post-industrial habitats. Plus Shropshire has a number of specialities which are not found anywhere else in the region (the Large Heath and Silver-studded Blue). If you add in beautiful landscapes, and rural areas with very low visitor numbers, it is easy to see why I fell in love with the place and why I quickly became an avid recorder of butterflies.

I was also fortunate in that the West Midlands Branch of Butterfly Conservation was very active and strong and it continues to be so today. The Branch runs an extensive programme of field trips as well as survey/monitoring training days and are happy to provide identification tips when necessary. After 12 summers of recording butterflies in Shropshire I had a good grasp of what the distribution and habitats of the key species were. By then I had also learnt much more about different aspects of butterfly life cycles. I had spent cold winter days using waders looking for Large Heath larvae on Fenn's and Whixall Mosses, had searched for Grayling larvae after dark on various areas of mine spoil in the Stiperstones area, and had spent hours watching three different sorts of fritillary (Dark Green Fritillary, Small Pearl-bordered Fritillary and Silver-washed Fritillary) both nectaring and egg laying.

Why is the recording and monitoring of butterflies important? They are very sensitive indicators of what is happening to the wider health of our countryside which is why Butterfly Conservation have successfully persuaded the UK government to accept butterflies and moths as Biodiversity Indicators. Mapping the distribution and abundance of butterflies and moths is also crucial as it allows Butterfly Conservation to concentrate its efforts where the need is greatest, as well as safeguarding and protecting the most vulnerable sites from development and damage. Continued fragmentation, deterioration and loss of wildlife habitats is also currently combined with the uncertainties of our changing climate. Butterflies respond quickly to climate change and the Butterfly Conservation datasets have already been able to show that at least 15 of our butterflies are now spreading further across the country.

Butterfly Conservation currently has two ongoing projects in Shropshire:

The Midlands Fritillary Project covers nine landscape areas in the West Midlands Region and currently has two strands in Shropshire. The first is a landscape project on the Wood White butterfly (a joint project with the Forestry Commission) and is being coordinated by Mike Williams. This project is aimed at increasing populations of the Wood White butterfly through targeted management at a landscape level in a number of woods across the Clun valley and near Ludlow. The second strand is survey and monitoring work on fritillaries (especially Small Pearl-bordered Fritillary and Dark Green Fritillary) which is being coordinated by Project Officer Nick Williams and involves local recorders. The aim here is for increased survey and monitoring effort to be followed up with management advice to maximize conservation benefits for fritillaries. These fritillaries are still fairly widespread in Shropshire (unlike so many other counties in the region) and we want to ensure their current status is maintained and enhanced in the county.

The Prees Heath Project (near Whitchurch in north Shropshire) is now in its fifth year with Stephen Lewis as its current warden. In 2010, at an emergence walk on 29th June those present saw several hundred Silver-studded Blues fluttering low over the heather and trefoil at the far end of the old airfield runway. In addition, at least 20 Silver-studded Blues were seen and photographed in the act of emergence, with black ants crawling over them to feed on sugary fluids, as the butterfly pumped up its wings before flying off to find a mate. Those familiar with the site will know that a major, long-term heathland re-creation project is ongoing on the former arable areas, in fact the biggest of its kind, using a soil inversion technique, in the UK. The Hangars Field is now showing large swathes of common heather, *Calluna vulgaris,* in flower less than three years after it was seeded by heather brash imported from Cannock Chase.

So plenty of butterfly related activities going on in Shropshire and plenty of scope for becoming involved. Do join Butterfly Conservation as by doing this you can make a real difference to the survival of butterflies, moths and their habitats. The more members we have the more we can achieve. Butterfly Conservation's strength derives from its 31 regional Branches, and the 14,500 members they embrace. The huge efforts of these Branch members currently enable Butterfly Conservation to monitor butterfly and moth activity throughout the British Isles. Public events are held all year round, including butterfly walks, moth events and countless conservation days. At present Shropshire is perhaps under-represented in the West Midlands Branch due to its rural nature so we are always looking for new members who are keen to take on an active role. The huge efforts undertaken by Nadia in pulling together this book show how just one dedicated person can make so much difference.

Jenny Joy

If you would like to learn more about Butterfly Conservation and the local West Midlands branch or wish to download a recording form for your sightings to send to us visit
www.butterfly-conservation.org.uk   or   www.westmidlands-butterflies.org.uk

As many of the activities of the West Midlands Branch of Butterfly Conservation are some distance away, Butterfly Conservation have recently set up a Shropshire Butterfly Group to focus on local activities and encourage more participation across the county. If you are interested in joining this group and receiving e-mail newsletters about Shropshire events please contact   jjoy@butterfly-conservation.org

Butterfly Conservation

Saving butterflies, moths and our environment

Towards Meaning

Butterflies, the souls of summer hours (John Masefield, *King Cole*)

Few elements of British wildlife can lead us further into the wonder of Nature than butterflies. They guide us into the heartland of our islands' most entrancing landscapes, when those places are at the zenith of their summertime beauty, and (at least theoretically) within the sanctity of sunshine. They offer pilgrimage into a reality where we may find true belonging, and where discovery and learning are ever present. The depth of experience is at times overwhelming. Perhaps this is what those of us who go 'butterflying', to use the Victorian term, are actually seeking?

Butterflying offers us far more than the release of serotonin and the satisfaction of the hunting gene. Each expedition is intrinsically unique, not least because the butterfly season changes almost daily. The effects of weather on butterflies, together with the variability of our climate and the ever-changing impacts of human actions, ensure that no two butterfly seasons are remotely alike. Butterflying continually reinvents itself, and build upon itself, iteratively.

Essentially, butterflies are spirits of time and place. Science has taught us precisely when and where to look, and how to look scientifically. But we need to look intuitively too, and learn how to record and understand not just our observations but our experiences - otherwise we have the experience but miss the meaning.

Then there are the bits today's butterfly enthusiasts rather ignore: - the immature stages. It is time to look afresh at metamorphosis, to search out the eggs, to understand the character and resilience of caterpillars and chrysalises, and to discover these creatures as symbols and metaphors within our own existence.

Science can hold us back, not of course from understanding butterflies as ecological subjects, but from understanding our relationship with them, and their significance to us. Only poetic language can describe the experience and meaning of butterflying, the layers of meaning - The poetic approach can also help us realise that conservation is essentially an expression of Love, albeit love rationalised through science.
.

That is why this book is important, and why, perhaps, the ancient Greeks used the same word, psyche, for both the butterfly and the soul, with Psyche herself being the goddess of the soul.

Matthew Oates

106

About the writers and artists

Jean Atkin lives with her family on a smallholding in Dumfries and Galloway, and writes on a corner of the kitchen dresser. Her poetry has been widely published and she has been a winner in several poetry competitions. Her short collection *The Treeless Region*, was published in 2010 by Ravenglass Poetry Press after she won a competition judged by John Burnside. She also has a pamphlet, *Lost At Sea*, Roncadora Press, published spring 2011.
Comma - **13** Purple Hairstreak - **68**

Rhys Bevan Jones works and researches in psychiatry in Cardiff, and is interested in the relationship between psychology/ psychiatry and the visual world. His work has been chosen for exhibitions in London and Wales, including the Association of Illustrators' Annual Exhibitions and the National Eisteddfod, and he has received a number of commissions for publications. Rhys has studied at Central St Martins and Kingston University, London.
Tree head - **91**

Sarah Bierley has lived in and around the Oswestry hills for nearly 20 years and once found a grayling perfectly camouflaged against the mottled rock from which her house was built. With fleabane and valerian, marjoram and michaelmas daisies, she has lured butterflies to her gardens. For many years she has also worked for Shropshire Wildlife Trust, writing and editing publications and press releases.
Farmland Butterflies - **98**

Pete Boardman has been involved in butterfly surveys for 20 years since moving down to Shropshire to work in the countryside. After 13 years working as a freelance ecologist / entomologist he took up a position with the Field Studies Council firstly running a project that encouraged others to get involved in biological recording, and now teaching entomological skills to volunteers.
Large Heath - **57** Verge-life - **99**

Ann Bridges often uses butterflies in her print-based paintings. Working from sketch-book studies she cuts and uses card stencils to create repeat patterns that so often occur in nature. Layers of inks are applied directly to the picture surface using small hand held rollers. By wiping off areas that are not quite dry and drawing into the ink, hidden colours are revealed and the richness of the image is gradually built up. www.ann-bridges.com
Orange-tip Butterflies - **16** Summer sunshine - **105**

Paul Brooks makes art where the final outcome is presented as a digital recording, he describes his work as 'meaning specific' where it can either take the form of video projection screened through shop windows or be sculptures located along a scenic trail. The work is often temporary. Some other projects can be seen at: www.millingtonwayposts.co.uk
http://www.bbc.co.uk/wear/content/articles/2008/01/28/sunniside_art_feature.shtml
Holly Blue - **18** Brimstone butter-coloured fly - **92**

Frances Carlile is a sculptor and printmaker. She trained at Camberwell and Chelsea schools of art. She has made a number of large scale sculptures in the landscape. Drawing and the natural world have always informed her work. *Butterfly Library* grew out of many hours spent in the Horniman Museum in South London, where the Lepidoptera collections are redolent with the dust of history.
Butterfly Library - **09** Butterfly Library, Peacock - **41**

Rita Carter studied art at The Royal Academy Schools. Her poetry appeared in *One For Jimmy*, edited by Matthew Sweeney; and magazines including Tandem, Fire and Obsessed With Pipework. She is a member of The Border Poets, Shropshire. *Along The Line*, and *Lodestones* are among publications, edited by Roger Garfitt, to which she contributed cover designs, sketches and poems; and a travelling exhibition to accompany *Leaves At The World's Edge.*
Wood Whites - **40**   Presences - **45**   Gatekeeper butterflies in lane - **65**   Peacock over stream - **81**
Orchard with Red Admirals - **101**

Keith Chandler is a recent migrant from Norfolk to Shropshire. Keith has had four collections of poems published by Carcanet, Peterloo and Redbeck. For further information please see his web site: *www.keithchandler.net*
Green Hairstreak **23**   Grayling **72**   Brimstone **93**

Gillian Clarke is a poet, playwright, translator (from Welsh), president of Ty Newydd, the Writers' Centre in North Wales, which she co-founded in 1990, and part time tutor in doctoral studies in Creative Writing, University of Glamorgan. She is the current National Poet for Wales. Recent books are a prose collection, *At the Source*, and a collection of poems, *A Recipe for Water*. She lives in Ceredigion.
A wind from Africa - **37**

Tim Clarke has remained stunned by the power potential of images, since first seeing drawings by Leonardo as a boy. That introduction has kept him motivated for almost forty years of practice. The painting shown derives from drawings made of dancers with special needs. Their body language, without hesitation or repetition, made him wonder if his creativity was capable of matching theirs.
Dancers with Green Hairstreak - **22**

Eleanor Cooke is a poet, whose collections include, *A Kind of Memory* (Seren), *Who Killed Prees Heath* (SWT and Bristol Classical Press), *Secret Files* (Jonathan Cape), and *The Return* (Salt). She has published short stories, and written for the stage and radio. For many years, Eleanor worked as a writer in schools, colleges, libraries, galleries (including Tate Liverpool) and in the community.
Prees Heath and the Silver-studded Blue - **96**

Jane Dards has had serious poetry published in magazines such as *Orbis*, *Iota*, *nthposition*, *Envoi* and *Seam*, with lighter work in the competition pages of *The Oldie* and *The Spectator*. She performs at local venues. Her first degree was in biology, and her PhD was on feral cats in Portsmouth Dockyard (www.feralcats.org.uk). She lives in an old house in the wilds of mid-Wales, and keeps a broomstick in the hall.
Speckled Wood - **20**

Paul Evans is a freelance writer, broadcaster and lecturer in nature writing at Bath Spa University. He writes for *The Guardian* as a country diarist on Wenlock Edge and contributes feature articles on wildlife and landscape issues to environmental periodicals. He is a writer and presenter of BBC Radio 4 programmes for the BBC's Natural History Unit including radio dramas. His background is in nature conservation and horticulture. He holds a PhD in philosophy and lives in Much Wenlock with his family.
Wenlock Edge - **95**

Giancarlo Facchinetti graduated from Wolverhampton University with a degree in fine art. Since then he has been involved in numerous exhibitions around Wolverhampton for which he has created sculpture, animation, film and text based art as well as experimental music. His underlying interests involve the exploration into the nature of reality. Currently living in the tranquillity of the countryside with his partner, he has focused his creativity towards making and recording his own music.
Meadow Brown - **80**

Pat Farrington worked first in publishing and then for BBC Schools Television making programmes for children, which included writing song lyrics. After leaving the BBC, she started writing poems for adults and has now had nine published. She writes poems mainly about how people interact with the natural environment, looking for 'portals' where closer connections can be made. Some of her poems have a wider message about threats to the environment.
Last Chance - **79**

Simon Fletcher was born in the Wyre Forest, Worcestershire, and is a freelance writer/ literature development officer. His first collection of poems from Pennine Pens, *The Occasions of Love*, was admired by Ted Hughes for 'the deft fluency, the economy, the pure tone, the pang'. He's also written *Nanny Knows Best!* (an e-novel), further collections of poetry and much journalism. He is currently the manager/editor of Offa's Press.
www.offaspress.co.uk
Silver-studded - **60** On Llynclys Common - **74**

Paul Francis has lived in Much Wenlock for thirty years. *Various Forms* contains a mixture of poems – rhymed and unrhymed, serious and comic, personal and political. 'I want readers to be intrigued and entertained; I don't want them to be baffled.'
He has won six poetry competitions, was third in the Guernsey Poetry on the Buses competition, and has two poems in the anthology *Emergency Verse*.
In pursuit of Butterflies - **07** Habitat - **39** Learning Curve - **44** White Admiral - **58** Blues - **63**

Lynette Forrester works with glass to explore interplay of light and colour, there is often a suggestion of fluidity and movement in her designs. Nature is a constant source of inspiration for her fused glass. Panels, screens, windows and garden sculptures are made in her studio near Ludlow. Lynette exhibits her work in galleries and selected garden sculpture venues. Commissions are undertaken with each individual client's wishes carefully considered. For more information about Lynette's work visit   www.glassdesignsuk.com
Butterflies in blue glass - **49**

Roger Garfitt lives in the Shropshire Hills, just below the Stone Age Ridgeway celebrated in the first of his *Border Songs*, which are engraved on glass screens in the County Archive in Shrewsbury. His *Selected Poems* are published by Carcanet and his memoir, *The Horseman's Word*, has just appeared from Jonathan Cape.
Wall - **32** Dark Green Fritillary - **52** Marbled White - **54** Red Admiral - **84**

Katy Goutefangea is an artist living and working in London. Since graduating in 2009 she has exhibited work in various venues including The Museum of Childhood, Bankside Gallery and Pushkin House. She works predominantly as a printmaker often using textiles in her practice. Her work explores themes of childhood, memory and folk mythology and seeks to combine the technical precision of printing with 'organic' media such as embroidery and crochet.   www.katyg.co.uk
Still Life - **90**   Still Life - **90**

Mavis Gulliver can't decide if she is a naturalist who writes poetry or a poet who is inspired by nature. Her poems which mainly focus on wildlife, landscape and islands have appeared in poetry magazines such as Envoi and Poetry Scotland; and in the 2010 'Grey Hen' anthology of bird poems, 'No Space But Their Own'. Many holidays have been spent in Shropshire but her home is on the Isle of Islay where she writes in a log cabin just ten metres from the sea.
Small Tortoiseshell - **09** Common Blue - **42** Large Skipper - **48**

Marilyn Gunn sees her poems as active meditation – ways of staying alive to the moment. From childhood she was drawn to watch and bear witness to the small forms and secret functions of the natural world. Born in 1944 in rural Sussex and now entirely settled in Shropshire she often writes sat on an up-turned bucket in her Broseley allotment. Nothing, she says, is ever too mean or plain for notice.
Small Copper - **27** The Large Whites' Waltz - **28** Gardeners' dilemma - **31** Poetry and Peacock - **41**
Meadow Browns' Gathering - **49** To a Meadow Brown - **80** The Peacock Winged Ones - **81**
Seasonal - **91**

Barbara Gunter-Jones is a textile artist who creates unique artworks by using the Victorian photographic technique of blueprinting. Plants or objects are placed directly onto treated cotton, silk, linen and wool and exposed onto the fabric using sunlight. The images are developed and tinted to create unusual effects. Barbara works on large-scale textile installations as well as illustrations and private commissions from her studio in Hertfordshire.
www.barbaragunterjones.co.uk
Bluebell ButterflyPhotogram - **11** Salvia Photogram - **67** Penstemon Photogram - **103**

Peter Holliday was born in Hereford and has lived in the Welsh Marches for the past forty years. He worked for the Library Service in Herefordshire and was Librarian at Leominster until retirement, lecturing regularly on local history. He joined the Border Poets and Ludlow Poets six years ago.
Small Tortoiseshell - 38 Wood White - 40

Julie Horner depicts wildlife; concentrating on butterflies, birds and small mammals from around her home in Cheshire. Her paintings are available as limited edition prints and greetings cards. Julie's butterfly paintings have been on the cover of the Welsh wildlife magazine Natur Cymru and featured in the wildlife edition of 'Artist and Illustrator'. Julie won the Amateur Category of 'Wildscape Wildlife Artist of the Year'. She edits the Shropshire Butterfly Group newsletter. www.butterflypaintings.co.uk   www.britishanimalpaintings.co.uk
Silver-studded Blue - **62** Red Admirals on plums - **82** Meadow Browns on buttercups - **99**

Sheilagh Jevons exhibits her work nationally. In 2007 she received Arts Council funding for an art walk installation on Wenlock Edge. In 2008 Sheilagh was invited to be one of the artist/curators for the Greenhouse Britain/Shropshire Exhibition at Shrewsbury Museum and Art Gallery. Her work endeavours to capture the atmosphere of a place, igniting a passion for the land that includes honouring all its inhabitants.
www.axisweb.org/artist/sheilaghjevons   www.cloudgallery.org
Butterfly Silver-studded Blue - **96** Butterfly Prees Heath - **97**

Jenny Joy grew up in Cambridge, went to Nottingham University to do a BSc in zoology followed by a PhD in animal behaviour which was completed in 1987. Arrived in Shropshire in 1990 after a spell in New Zealand. Spent 12 years working on various survey and research projects on butterflies then joined Butterfly Conservation as a member of staff in 2002. Was promoted to Senior Regional Officer in 2007.
A personal perspective on Shropshire Butterflies - **104**

Nadia Kingsley has made brick sculpture, textile art and photographic works, since her ceramics degree in 2001; and has been exhibited in Birmingham, London and Brighton. She grows vegetables and sends in recordings for Butterfly Conservation. Nadia has won prizes for short stories, and her poems have been published in Brand, Orbis, The Comma and Field Studies Council magazines; and the 2011 anthology of Wenlock Poetry Festival.
The First butterflies of Spring - **10** Viewpoint - **15** Dingy Skipper - **26** Pearl-bordered Fritillary - **35**
Stiperstones Valentine - **46** Silver-washed Fritillary - **66** Red for Danger - **77**

Chris Kinsey was BBC Wildlife Poet of the Year in 2008. Ragged Raven Press has published two poetry collections: *Kung Fu Lullabies* and *Cure for a Crooked Smile*. She writes a regular nature diary for Cambria and occasional articles for Natur Cymru and The Western Mail. Chris' greyhounds are accomplices to wildlife sightings. Her first two plays have had readings at Aberystwyth Arts Centre and with The National Theatre.
Red Admirals in September - **83** From the Hibernaculum of the Small Skippers - **89**

Ellen McBride grew up in a farming village and now interprets the countryside in its various guises. She moved to Scotland to study at the Scottish College of Textiles, where she learnt the value of observational drawing, colour, pattern and texture. Perhaps a little illogically she then went on to work alongside ecologists, thus returning her focus to the rural setting. Ellen works as an artist, freelance writer and project coordinator.
Orange-tip - Underwing - **17** Large Heath - Grey Pilgrim - **56** Brown Argus - Fine Line - **76**
Red Admiral - Missing parts - **85** Orange-tip flight - **98**

Alwyn Marriage has had six books published. These include poetry and non-fiction. She has read at many festivals and events in Britain and abroad, and her poetry appears frequently in magazines and anthologies. Alwyn has been a university lecturer, Editor of a journal, Chief Executive of two international NGOs and an environmental consultant. She is now Managing Editor of Oversteps Books and research fellow at Surrey University. Her mother came from Clun.   www.marriages.me.uk
September Butterfly - **78**

Adrian Miles became fascinated by the beauty of butterflies and moths during a long hot summer holiday spent in a family cottage in Montgomeryshire. He noticed a gold-speckled object hanging in the beech hedge bordering the garden path. This was put into a kilner jar, and days later a small tortoiseshell butterfly had emerged. He plays an active role in conservation in Shropshire and is chairman of the Haycop conservation group, Broseley.
Large White laying eggs on nasturtium - **29** Pearl-bordered Fritillary - **35** Large Skipper - **48**
White-letter Hairstreak - **70** Small Skipper - **89**

Paola Minekov has a view of the world which is rich in emotion and she captures relationships with a heartbeat of love, lust, and misunderstandings. In her cityscapes she reveals her memories and visions of the cities we live in. The paintings in her *Dancers Series* are renowned for their vibrant colours and the lively atmosphere they evoke. Paola lives and works in London and exhibits both nationally and internationally. For more information please visit   www.paolaminekov.com
Spring - **12**

Lis Molzahn has worked across a variety of media and likes to introduce an element of surprise, intrigue or irony into her work so the viewer may question what they are looking at. Recent work often consists of making and photographing small objects, and can be seen at www.lismolzahn.moonfruit.com. Lis has also collaborated in projects where community involvement plays an integral role.
Butterfly Net - **31** Wall Butterfly - **33**

Chris Morgan was Birmingham's Poet Laureate 2008-9. The author or editor of ten books, he's had a lifelong interest in butterflies and moths, pursuing and photographing them in Britain and abroad. His day job is teaching creative writing to adults, and he lectures on a wide range of wildlife, art and literary topics to U3A, W.I. and similar groups.
Chris@pandcmorgan.demon.co.uk
Prees Heath - **62**

Pauline Morgan is a retired teacher. She has been runner up in a couple of poetry competitions and has had short stories published professionally. She reviews books on the on-line website *SFcrowsnest*, and was a judge for the Arthur C. Clarke award for Science Fiction. She enjoys gardening and wildlife activities, especially related to bats and butterflies being a member of the relevant conservation groups. She can be contacted at Pauline@pandcmorgan.demon.co.uk
White Letter Day - **70**

Adrian Moule is a painter and printmaker working in the North East. Common Blues was produced whilst working on Green TV, in partnership with Tees Valley Arts and Heritage Lottery Fund.
Common Blue - **42**

Linda Nevill is an artist, BA Hons MA Hons, who explores her passions for wildlife, plants and gardens, travel, light and colour through the prints and paintings that she creates. She is fascinated by the unpredictability of process and the pursuing of an idea. Linda has studied in the UK, Albuquerque and New York and participated in numerous exhibitions. She is co-founder and Chair of Imagetextimage, a group of artists that collaborate to produce contemporary art and poetry.   www.lindanevill.com
www.imagetextimage.com
Ringlet - **55** Comma - **78**

Wendy Newhofer makes kiln formed glass. She creates expressive pieces often using familiar images which are transformed by a change of scale. A combination of glass and metal in the form of fine leaf and wire enables her to 'draw' within the glass. This produces a palette of subtle colours with a real painterly quality when the glass is fired in the kiln.
Clouded Yellow - **44**

Patricia Newland started writing poetry as the New Millennium began. Her poems are mainly philosophical, religious or with a touch of humour in content. When her husband, David, began photographing butterflies, she often accompanied him. This led her to be enthusiastic about the beauty and nature of butterflies. Some of Patricia's poetry is in David's book *Discover Butterflies in Britain* published by WildGuides. Her book *Colours of Christ* can be obtained from her: patricia.newland@gmail.com
Brimstone - **11** Holly Blue - **18** Green Hairstreak - **22** Common Blues - **43** Ringlets - **55**

Matthew Oates became captivated by butterflies and poetry at Christ's Hospital school in the West Sussex countryside. An English graduate, he is recognised as an authority on butterflies and their conservation, though he only admits to being a pilgrim in the world of Nature. He has worked as a senior ecologist for the National Trust since 1990, and is also a writer and broadcaster on wildlife and nature.
On seeing the first Orange-tip - **16** On Whixhall Moss ... - **57** Camilla of the Brambles - **59**
Amongst the Heather - **62** Evening Flight - **68** Towards Meaning - **106**

Miriam Obrey lives in rural Shropshire. Her poems appear in magazines including The North, The Rialto, Quadrant, Smiths Knoll, Warwick University literary magazine and Oxford Poets Anthology 2007. She was the winner of *Precious Earth* poetry competition, Ludlow 2011.
Wood White butterflies - **40**

Robert Offord is a multi media artist. He was born, educated and has lived his life in London. The Orange-tip butterfly featured in this boxed construction was found by a friend in her Oxford garden, and presented to him so that he could make something magical. 'The world is a speck of stone spinning in space. Do what you can before the day is done.'
Orange-tip Diary - **17**

Nick Pearson is a poet who lives in Shropshire. His work has appeared in magazines and anthologies. His collection *Made in Captivity* is forthcoming from Offa's Press in 2011.
Small Heath - **34** Small Tortoiseshell - **90**

Mario Petrucci is an ecologist, physicist and educator, "one of the best poets of our times" (*Literati Magazine*). Recipient of the prestigious Arvon and Bridport prizes, and four times winner of the London Writers competition, he is the only poet to have been in residence at the Imperial War Museum and with BBC Radio 3. *i tulips* (Enitharmon, 2010) has been hailed by the Poetry Book Society as a "truly ambitious landmark body of work". www.mariopetrucci.com
Lepidoptera XIII - **14** Lepidoptera IX - **30** Lepidoptera I - **67**

Hilary Portman was born in North Wales in 1961 and now lives with her family in Somerset. A nurse for 28 yrs, she has maintained her lifelong interest in art, crafts and natural history, culminating in 2010 in an Hons degree combining these subjects. She now hopes to change career and to use her creative ability to highlight both the beauty and concerns that affect our landscapes and wildlife today.
Ragwort - **15** Green-veined White butterfly - **25** Essex Skipper - **50** Marbled White - **54**

Emma Purshouse is a writer and performance poet. She performs her work across the UK at festivals and spoken word nights. Emma has completed poetry residencies for Wolverhampton Libraries, The New Vic Theatre in Stoke-on-Trent and has been a visiting poet for Ledbury Poetry Festival Schools' Programme. A CD of Emma's poetry, entitled *Upsetting the Applecart*, was released by Offa's Press in 2010.   www.offaspress.co.uk
Comma - **13** When the attention span is smaller than the wing span ... - **19** Out of Essex - **51**

Adrian M Riley was born in Birmingham in 1958. Moved to Shropshire in 1962. As Lepidoptera recorder there, he published two books. In 1979 he moved to Hertfordshire, became Head of the national moth survey for Rothamsted Research, rose to Higher Scientific Officer and published around 150 papers and a book on moths. After early retirement in 2002 he has published three further books on butterflies and birdwatching. He now writes and guides on wildlife tours.
Reminiscences of 'The Silver-haired Man': A Shropshire Old Lad - **102**

Jane Seabourne was born in Wales and now lives in Wolverhampton. She is a member of ImageTextImage, a collective of writers and artists who exhibit and perform their work throughout the West Midlands . Jane's poems have been published in a wide range of national journals. She recently co-edited the anthology, *New Writings from Wolverhampton*. Jane's debut collection of poems, *Bright Morning*, was published by Offa's Press in 2010.
Regarding the Green-veined White - **24** The Uncommon Common Blue - **43**

Ruth Stacey spends her time wrestling with poems and three small children who will not put their coats on to play in the garden. She is currently completing a Masters in Literature and writes poetry in the spaces between motherhood and walking the dog. Based in Worcestershire, she fiercely loves her rural heritage and the surrounding countryside. She reads compulsively and loves history books which often inspire her poetry.
Hedge Brown - **64**

Kim Stephens graduated in 2009 from Norwich Art School covering a room with large inky drawings of anthropomorphic wasps for the final show. She has since been exhibiting in Norwich; her most recent work is inspired by the characteristics that earn animals their collective nouns. When not drawing, she studies the art of beekeeping and floristry, discovering they all inspire each other. To see more work, or to contact Kim regarding commissions visit   www.kimrebecca.blogspot.com
Grizzled Skipper Caterpillar - **19** Small Copper - **27** Painted Lady - **36** Dark Green Fritillary - **53** Silver-studded Blue - **61**

Jeremy Stretton is a Shropshire lad. Born 1955, Ironbridge, son of Lionel, Beryl, the soil and the Severn . Spent the best of subsequent years listening to, watching and smiling at the power and glory of nature in all its forms . Guilty butterfly collector of 1960s, lizard conservator, Wenlock limestone fossil collector, catch-and-release fisher, grain trader, drystone waller, raspberry lover. Proud father, grandfather with a love of all, and quietness.
Large White - **30**

Katherine Swift came to live at the Dower House, Morville Hall, in 1988, abandoning a career as a rare book librarian in Oxford and Dublin, to make a garden. That garden was the subject of her first book, *The Morville Hours*. Her second, *The Morville Year*, is based on the gardening column she wrote for the *Times* newspaper in 2001-2005. It was published in March 2011.
Gardens and Butterflies - **100**

Bill Thomas is a teacher, poet & preacher based in Hereford. His poems have appeared on Guernsey buses and at Greenbelt, though more often at readings in Hereford-shire & Monmouthshire. He started photographing butterflies thirty years ago, but has recently switched to letter boxes, as they don't move so fast. A selection of poems appears at www.woodenheadarts.com, & he can be contacted for performances at emeraldpenguin@hotmail.com
Imago - **88**

Carl Thompson is an award winning British artist and illustrator. His portfolio of work ranges from portraiture to still life, it is however as a wildlife artist that Carl has a growing national and international reputation. A selection of his work is now available as limited edition prints and greetings cards. Carl is happy to accept both private and commercial commissions.   www.airartbycarl.co.uk   email: carl@airartbycarl.co.uk
 telephone: 01584 823541
Speckled Wood and Bramble - **21** Small 'Tortoise' and Buddleia - **86**

Debs Thurkettle is in the 2nd year of a BA Hons Degree in Fine Art Painting at Bath Spa University. Her primary area of focus is in the use of colour, as a means of examining the environment around - from the smallest insect or a seed pod - to greater 'scapes' of the sky, wind, and rain - and investigating how these affect the body, mind and senses.
Wing - **14** Blue Drift - **75**

Janet Vernon is originally from North West London. She moved to Shropshire twenty years ago. She has always felt an empathy with the natural world, finding inspiration in all its different moods. She counts herself lucky to live within walking distance of Prees Heath Common (the last sanctuary in the English Midlands for the Silver-studded Blue butterfly) with her partner Malcolm and a cat called Cussypat.
Orange-tip - **17** Greenfields - **25** The Heath - morning time - **61**

Ben Waddams is a wildlife artist working in oils and pen & ink. His fascination for the natural world has brought him endless joy since before he can remember. Today he works in the media and with charities in an effort to preserve the wildlife he is so fond of and his aim is to inspire an appreciation of natural history through his art, more of which can be seen here: www.waddams.webs.com
Silver-washed Fritillary - **66** Grayling - **73** Silver-washed Fritillary - **95**

Jamila Walker is a Shropshire based Visual Artist and Art Worker. The formal aspects where Jamila's interests lie are colour and texture. Jamila's practice is inspired by many aspects of life from nature, to found objects, to stories. Jamila has exhibited her work widely and features in Art Magazines, Art Books and on Fashion bags.
www.jamilawalker.webeden.co.uk
Butterfly Clouds - **107**

Neil Webb works in colour pencil and gouache, which enables him to represent effervescent colour and precise detail. He has a passion for nature and the outdoors and has travelled to many beautiful parts of the world since finishing his degree at Falmouth College of Arts. Neil lives in Brighton and takes inspiration from his surroundings on the south coast of England whilst walking, cycling, surfing and more.
Clouded Yellow on Foxgloves - **01** Bird's-foot Trefoil - **26** Sweet Violet - **119**

Tom Wentworth has been published in various magazines, journals and online. Currently he continues to be a columnist for Able Magazine and is developing an Afternoon Play. He somehow finds time to study BA Radio at the University of Glamorgan and is also a member of Bridgnorth Writers' Group. He is thrilled to be contributing to this anthology.
The Gatekeeper - **64** White Letter Hairstreak - **71**

Lynn Wheeler is a talented artist and illustrator. Originally from Oxford, she studied graphics and illustration at Hull and then went on to teach Art & Design in Dorset. In 1986 Lynn relocated to Cheshire and has pursued a busy career in IT designing learning materials, producing marketing collateral and commercial websites. She is delighted to have the opportunity to create illustrations for inspirational projects such as this book.
Dingy Skipper - **26** Nettle and Small Tortoiseshell larvae - **39**

Christine Wilcox-Baker draws inspiration from re-connecting man with nature. Her practice encompasses exploration, experimentation, research, heritage, sustainability, and responses to surroundings and situations. Always a passionate gardener and artist she has become increasingly influenced by food cultivation with its inherent value and beauty. She works on commissioned installations, paintings, drawings and photography, in solo and collaborative projects. 07836 22884   www.axisweb.org/artist/christinewilcoxbaker
Small Heath - **34** Small Pearl-bordered Fritillary - **47** Purple Hairstreaks - **69**

Kiran Williams is a print artist exploring print and dye processes across paper and fabric. Producing decorative textiles designed to merge interior and exterior landscapes. Artwork combines characteristics drawn from cloth landscapes of folds and fibres with external landscapes of light and shadow. Drawing and paper print processes also contribute to illustrative pieces, inspiring floral, foliate and insect imagery. www.kiranlee.co.uk kiranleetextiles.blogspot.com
White Admiral - **59**

Charles Worth is a member of Bridgnorth Writers' Group. He has lived in Newport, Shropshire, for nearly thirty years. Brought up in London, he taught in secondary schools in Bristol and has worked for Christian Aid and the Methodist Church. Charles's passions and pursuits include family and friends, walking the South West Coast Path, exploring psychological type theory, chairing his local environmental action group and working with asylum-seekers in Birmingham.
Small Tortoiseshell - **87**

Contents and their Creators